D1271791

Valentine

God's Courageous Evangelist

VOM
BOOKS

Valentine: God's Courageous Evangelist

VOM Books
1815 SE Bison Rd.
Bartlesville, OK 74006

ISBN 978-0-88264-205-5

Written by The Voice of the Martyrs with Cheryl Odden

Illustrated by R. F. Palavicini

Printed in the United States of America

For our Christian brothers and sisters
around the world today who, like Valentinus,
know obeying God is worth the risk

A Note to Parents and Educators

Valentine's Day is celebrated every year on February 14, but why? Many buy cards and candy hearts as expressions of love, unaware there was a man named Valentine. Who was the man behind this holiday that has become known for Cupid, chocolate, roses, and love notes saying "Be my Valentine"?

Valentinus, or St. Valentine as he would come to be known, was a leader in the church and lived in the Roman Empire during the third century. However, there are three "Valentines" who lived in the late third century during Emperor Claudius II's reign. One was a priest in Rome, another a bishop of Interamna (modern Italy), and the third a martyr in a Roman province of Africa. Some believe the martyrdom of all three men named Valentinus occurred on February 14. Many scholars believe two of them, the priest in Rome and the bishop of Interamna, are the same, suggesting a Roman priest became the bishop of Interamna who was sentenced there and brought to Rome for his execution. It is believed Valentinus' martyrdom occurred about the year AD 269.

Many would agree the life of Valentinus is a mystery, though some have even questioned his existence. History proved his existence, however, when archaeologists unearthed a Roman catacomb and an ancient church dedicated to him. He is mentioned in Jacobus de Voragine's *Golden Legend*, written about saints around the year 1260. (It is noted this was perhaps the most widely read book after the Bible during the late Middle Ages.) He was also featured in a woodcut in the illustrated book *The Nuremberg Chronicle,* printed in 1493.

Sources indicate Emperor Claudius II had Valentinus executed for secretly marrying Roman soldiers, defying the emperor's order that soldiers were not to wed. Claudius (also called "Claudius the Cruel") was having difficulty recruiting men and believed it was because soldiers, required to fight for at least twenty-five years, were unwilling to leave their loved ones. Therefore, Claudius banned all marriages and engagements. However, Valentinus secretly married couples

4

until he was caught and brought before the Prefect of Rome. It is even believed Valentinus tried to convert Emperor Claudius. In *Valentine: God's Courageous Evangelist*, the conversation between Emperor Claudius and Valentinus is based on the one printed in de Voragine's *Golden Legend*. Another legend says during Valentinus' imprisonment, while awaiting his execution, he restored the sight of his jailer's daughter. (In this story we call the jailer "Marcus.") Yet another says on the eve of his death, he wrote a note to the jailer's daughter and signed it, "From your Valentine."

In AD 496, more than two hundred years after Valentinus was executed, a church leader marked February 14 as a celebration to honor Valentinus' courageous life. This was to replace a pagan Roman holiday. February 14 was the day the Romans honored Juno, the queen of the Roman gods and goddesses, who was also known as the goddess of women and marriage. The following day, February 15, started the Feast of Lupercalia, which honored Faunus, the god of fertility and forests. On the eve of Lupercalia, the names of Roman girls were written on paper and placed in jars. Young men would draw a girl's name and be partnered with that girl throughout the festival. Sometimes this pairing lasted the whole year, and often they would fall in love and later marry.

And what about Cupid? Why does his image appear during Valentine's Day? Cupid was the Roman god of love.

Despite the mystery, legends, and questions masking the man Valentine, this story was written to convey his courageous life and death. May *Valentine: God's Courageous Evangelist* inspire children of all ages to boldly present Jesus Christ to a world in need of His hope (1 Peter 3:15)!

6

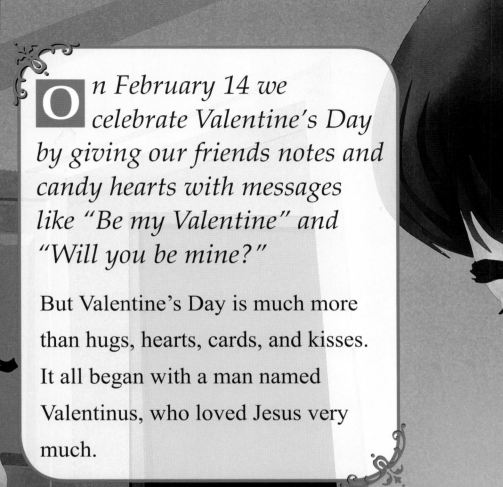

On February 14 we celebrate Valentine's Day by giving our friends notes and candy hearts with messages like "Be my Valentine" and "Will you be mine?"

But Valentine's Day is much more than hugs, hearts, cards, and kisses. It all began with a man named Valentinus, who loved Jesus very much.

GREAT BRITAIN

FRANCE

SPAIN

ROME

GREECE

SPQR

NORTH AFRICA

MEDITERRAN

Valentinus was born more than two hundred years after Jesus' birth, in a land called the Roman Empire.

The Roman Empire was so big it stretched all the way across Europe and parts of East and North Africa. It was also very powerful, conquering any tribe that dared to invade its territory.

TURKEY

N

YPT

9

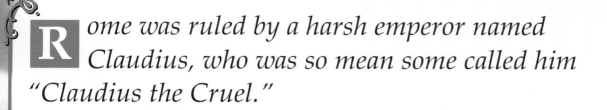

Rome was ruled by a harsh emperor named *Claudius, who was so mean some called him "Claudius the Cruel."*

Claudius was a tall man and had eyes of fire. Many said he was so strong he could knock the teeth out of a man or an animal with just one punch. Claudius was also very skilled in battle and conquered the tribes that tried to invade the Roman Empire, but more and more tribes were becoming a threat. "We need more soldiers to defeat the barbaric invaders!" complained Claudius. So began his search for strong, young men to fight with him.

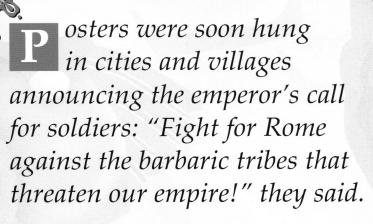

P osters were soon hung in cities and villages announcing the emperor's call for soldiers: *"Fight for Rome against the barbaric tribes that threaten our empire!"* they said.

But few men responded to the emperor's call for soldiers. They knew they would have to leave behind their loved ones—their wives, mothers, fathers, children, or the women they had promised to marry—and wouldn't see them for at least twenty-five years.

Claudius became very angry that few men wanted to become soldiers, so he decided to create a new law. "There will be no weddings in Rome!" declared Claudius the Cruel.

The people of Rome could not believe what they had just heard! "No weddings?" they cautiously whispered in their homes and on the streets. "How could the emperor do such a thing?" Young men and women engaged to be married were heartbroken. "Now what do we do?" they cried.

There was a church leader who was also surprised and saddened by the emperor's new rule. His name was Valentinus.

Valentinus was very troubled. *"Marriage was God's idea, and no emperor can hinder what God created! If we choose to marry couples secretly, we could go to prison,"* said Valentinus to Marius, who served with him in the church.

The people of Rome already knew Valentinus and Marius would not worship the Roman gods. "This could get us into more trouble," they agreed. But they decided obeying God was worth the risk.

So deep in the woods, under the cover of midnight's darkness, couples would meet Valentinus to be joined in marriage.

But it wasn't long before news of Valentinus' secret wedding ceremonies reached the ear of Emperor Claudius.

"Arrest the traitor Valentinus at once!" he ordered his guards, who found Valentinus and dragged him before the emperor.

19

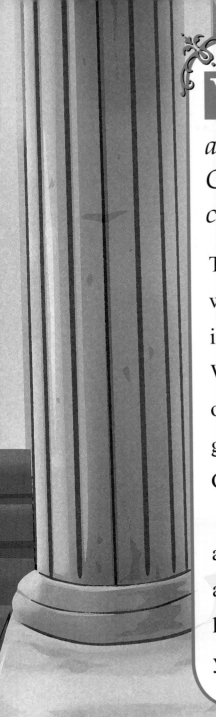

Valentinus' ankles and wrists were put in chains as he stood before Emperor Claudius and members of the court.

The emperor looked fiercely at this man who disobeyed his law and said, "What is this I have heard of you, Valentinus? Why will you not live in peace by obeying my laws, worshiping the Roman gods, and turning your back on your God?"

Valentinus looked up at the emperor and said for all to hear, "If you knew about the grace of God, you wouldn't have asked me to deny Him and worship your idols!"

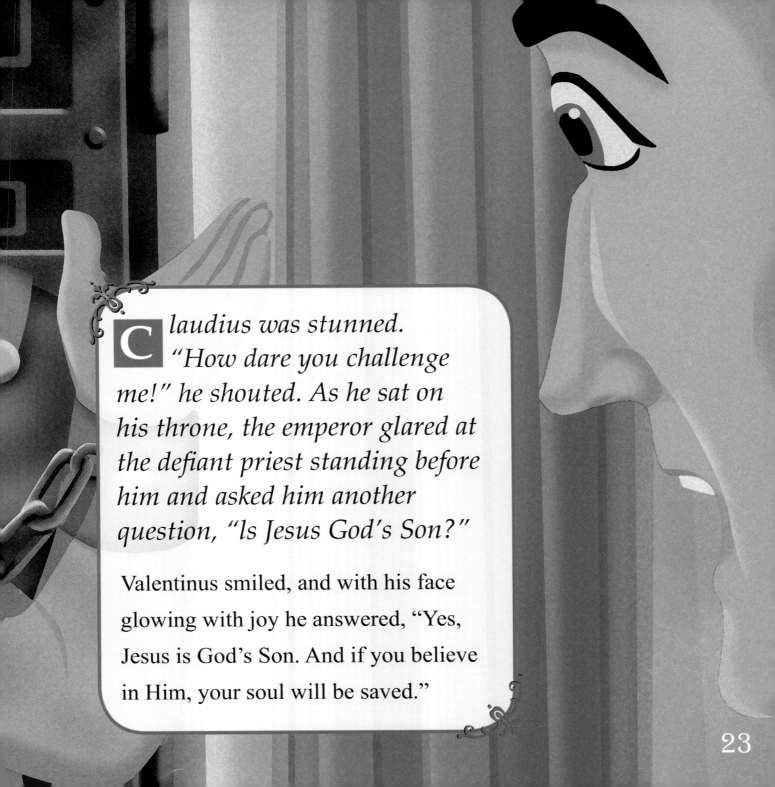

Claudius was stunned. "How dare you challenge me!" he shouted. As he sat on his throne, the emperor glared at the defiant priest standing before him and asked him another question, "Is Jesus God's Son?"

Valentinus smiled, and with his face glowing with joy he answered, "Yes, Jesus is God's Son. And if you believe in Him, your soul will be saved."

Claudius sat on his throne and thought hard about what Valentinus had just said. Suddenly, Claudius stood up and exclaimed, "This man's words made sense! What is wrong with asking Jesus to save our souls?"

The chief prison guard named Marcus stood up and said, "Emperor, you are being misled by the words of this criminal. Why should we turn our backs on worshiping the Roman gods when this is what we've been taught since we were children?"

Claudius changed his mind and cried, "Take this criminal away! He is to be put to death for breaking my laws!"

Marcus grabbed Valentinus by the arm and led him to his prison cell.

Marcus took the rusty iron key from his belt and turned the lock on the cell door, throwing Valentinus onto the cold, hard, dirt floor.

But Valentinus knew he was not defeated. He had just told the emperor, Claudius the Cruel, about Jesus Christ. Even the court officials heard. *He rejected Jesus' free gift of salvation,* Valentinus sadly thought. *But maybe someday he will accept it.*

O ne day while Marcus was standing guard, Valentinus began to pray, "Lord Jesus, You are light. Fill this prison with Your light in such a way that those who are here will know You are God."

When Marcus heard his prayer, he turned toward Valentinus and said, "You say God is light. My daughter has been blind since birth. If your God can make her see, then I will believe in your God."

So Valentinus prayed God would cause his daughter's blind eyes to see.

The next morning Valentinus was awakened by the sound of feet hitting the hard earth.

As soon as he sat up on his straw mat, he saw Marcus grabbing the bars of his cell and shaking them. "She can see!" Marcus exclaimed. "My daughter can see!" And he and his entire family decided to believe in Jesus.

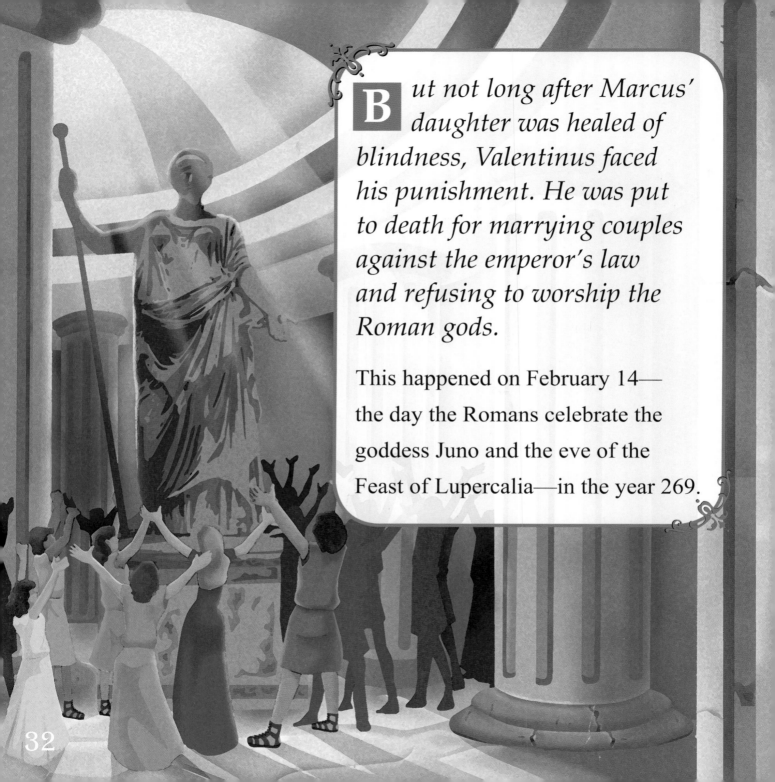

But not long after Marcus' daughter was healed of blindness, Valentinus faced his punishment. He was put to death for marrying couples against the emperor's law and refusing to worship the Roman gods.

This happened on February 14—the day the Romans celebrate the goddess Juno and the eve of the Feast of Lupercalia—in the year 269.

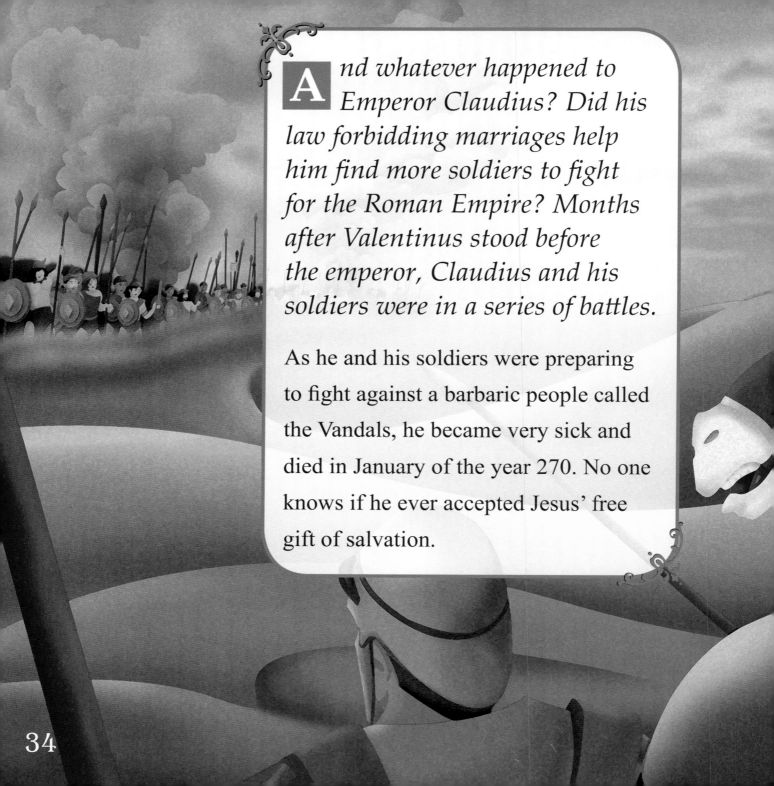

A nd whatever happened to Emperor Claudius? Did his law forbidding marriages help him find more soldiers to fight for the Roman Empire? Months after Valentinus stood before the emperor, Claudius and his soldiers were in a series of battles.

As he and his soldiers were preparing to fight against a barbaric people called the Vandals, he became very sick and died in January of the year 270. No one knows if he ever accepted Jesus' free gift of salvation.

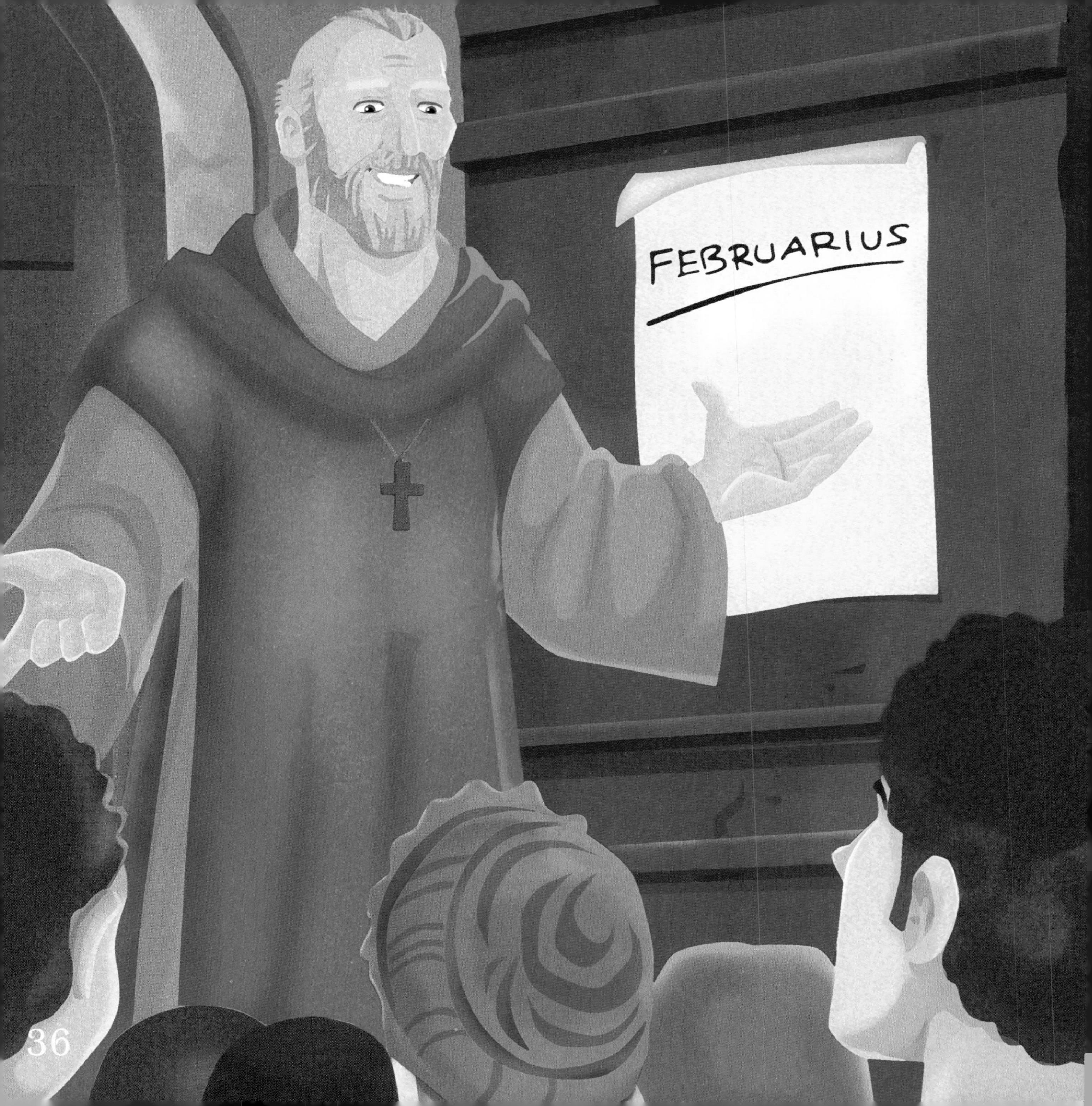
FEBRUARIUS

A lmost two hundred years after Valentinus died, a leader in the church declared February 14 to be the day Christians honor and remember the courageous life of Valentinus.

This replaced the Roman holiday that celebrated the goddess Juno and the eve of the Feast of Lupercalia.

There are countries today where Christians cannot legally gather together and worship.

If they are caught having a Bible study, prayer meeting, or baptism outside the buildings where the government allows them to meet, they are often arrested. Like Valentinus, these Christians use this opportunity to share the gospel with the police who have arrested them.

In Vietnam, a woman named Vu (pronounced "voo") was arrested for attending a prayer meeting in the mountains.

When the police questioned her, she told them how Jesus died on the cross so they could be forgiven. Suddenly, four more police who had been listening from a nearby room entered. One of them asked, "If we want to believe in God, is it possible?" She said, "Yes, anytime."

Vu was arrested many more times. Each time, a different policeman was sent to question her, because officials were afraid she would convince them to trust in Jesus.

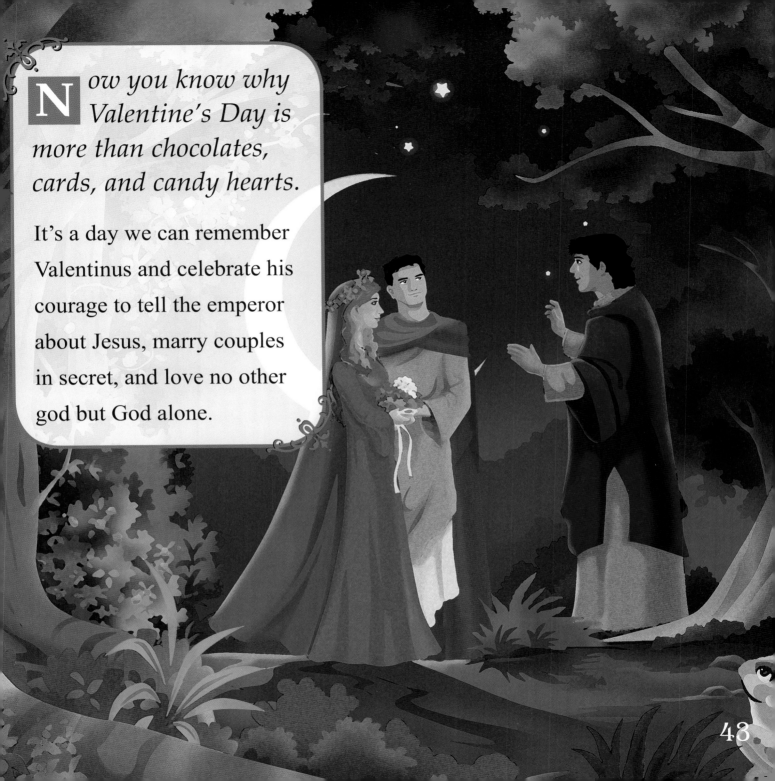

Now you know why Valentine's Day is more than chocolates, cards, and candy hearts.

It's a day we can remember Valentinus and celebrate his courage to tell the emperor about Jesus, marry couples in secret, and love no other god but God alone.

For Reflection

"You will be brought before governors and kings for My sake, as a testimony to them and to the Gentiles. But when they deliver you up, do not worry about how or what you should speak. For it will be given to you in that hour what you should speak."
(Matthew 10:18,19)

What does Jesus promise in these verses?

What did Valentinus say when he was brought before the emperor and the court officials?

How did Jesus' words in these verses come true in Valentinus' life?

What would you say if someone asked you why you go to church, pray before your meal, or take your Bible to school?

Prayer

Lord Jesus, thank You for Your promise to give us the words to speak when we are questioned about our faith in You. Give me opportunities, like Valentinus, to boldly and graciously declare that You are God and that You give us hope and purpose in this life. Thank You for Christians like Valentinus and others around the world today who inspire us through their courageous stand for You as they refuse to bow to idols in exchange for an easier life.
Amen.

Bibliography

"Claudius II." *The Columbia Encyclopedia,* 6th ed. (New York: Columbia University Press, 2003). Accessed 5 January 2006. <www.answers.com/topic/claudius-ii>.

"'Claudius II Gothicus,' Marcus Aurelius Valerius Claudius (AD 214–AD 270)." *Illustrated History of the Roman Empire.* Accessed 5 January 2006. <www.roman-empire.net/decline/claudius-II.html>.

de Voragine, Jacobus, and William Granger Ryan (trans.). *The Golden Legend: Readings on the Saints, Volume 1* (Princeton, NJ: Princeton University Press, 1993).

"The History of Saint Valentine's Day." Accessed 5 January 2006. <www.pictureframes.co.uk/pages/saint_valentine.htm>.

"Lupercalia." *The Columbia Encyclopedia*, 6th ed. Accessed 5 January 2006. <www.encyclopedia.com/html/l/lupercal.asp>.

"The Roman Army," *The Romans*. BBC Schools Programme. Accessed 5 January 2006. <www.bbc.co. uk/schools/romans/army.shtml>.

"Saint Valentine's Day." *The Columbia Encyclopedia*, 6th ed. Accessed 5 January 2006. <www.encyclopedia.com/html/s/stv1alent.asp>.

"St. Valentine." Catholic Online. Accessed 5 January 2006. <www.catholic.org/saints/saint.php?saint_id=159>.

"St. Valentine." *The Catholic Encyclopedia, Volume XV* (New York: Robert Appleton Company, 1912).

Weigel, Richard D. "Claudius II Gothicus (268–270)." *An Online Encyclopedia of Roman Emperors.* Accessed 5 January 2006. <www.roman-emperors.org/claudgot.htm>.

"What Happened This Day in Church History, February 14, 269, Martyrdom of St. Valentine." Christian History Institute. Accessed 5 January 2006. <www.chi.gospelcom.net/chi/DAILYF/2002/02/daily-02-14-2002.shtml>.

The Voice of the Martyrs is a Christian nonprofit organization dedicated to helping those who are persecuted for their Christian witness in Communist, Islamic, and other nations hostile to Christ. In 1967, after being ransomed from Communist Romania, Richard and Sabina Wurmbrand came to the US and began their ministry to the persecuted church. Their vision was global, and a network of offices was birthed to raise awareness of, and take relief to, those suffering for their Christian witness.

For a free monthly newsletter and ways you can help today's persecuted church, contact:

The Voice of the Martyrs
1815 SE Bison Rd.
Bartlesville, OK 74006
(800) 747-0085
E-mail: thevoice@vom.org
Website: persecution.com
Youth website: kidsofcourage.com